AF490445

THIS BOOK BELONGS TO

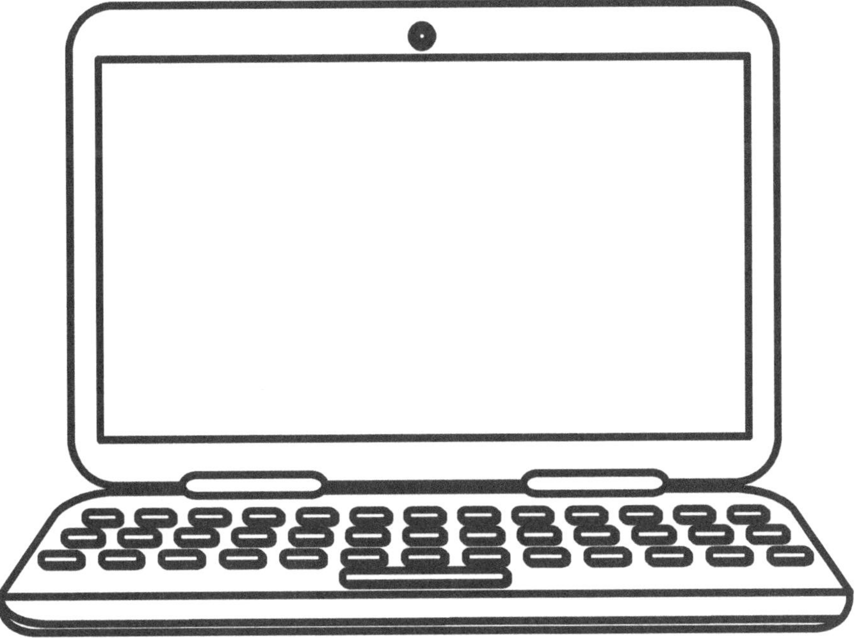

A

WEBSITE	
USERNAME	
PASSWORD	
NOTE	

WEBSITE	
USERNAME	
PASSWORD	
NOTE	

WEBSITE	
USERNAME	
PASSWORD	
NOTE	

WEBSITE	
USERNAME	
PASSWORD	
NOTE	

WEBSITE	
USERNAME	
PASSWORD	
NOTE	

WEBSITE	
USERNAME	
PASSWORD	
NOTE	

WEBSITE	
USERNAME	
PASSWORD	
NOTE	

WEBSITE	
USERNAME	
PASSWORD	
NOTE	

WEBSITE	
USERNAME	
PASSWORD	
NOTE	

WEBSITE	
USERNAME	
PASSWORD	
NOTE	

WEBSITE	
USERNAME	
PASSWORD	
NOTE	

WEBSITE	
USERNAME	
PASSWORD	
NOTE	

WEBSITE	
USERNAME	
PASSWORD	
NOTE	

WEBSITE	
USERNAME	
PASSWORD	
NOTE	

WEBSITE	
USERNAME	
PASSWORD	
NOTE	

A

WEBSITE	
USERNAME	
PASSWORD	
NOTE	

WEBSITE	
USERNAME	
PASSWORD	
NOTE	

WEBSITE	
USERNAME	
PASSWORD	
NOTE	

WEBSITE	
USERNAME	
PASSWORD	
NOTE	

WEBSITE	
USERNAME	
PASSWORD	
NOTE	

B

WEBSITE	
USERNAME	
PASSWORD	
NOTE	

WEBSITE	
USERNAME	
PASSWORD	
NOTE	

WEBSITE	
USERNAME	
PASSWORD	
NOTE	

WEBSITE	
USERNAME	
PASSWORD	
NOTE	

WEBSITE	
USERNAME	
PASSWORD	
NOTE	

WEBSITE	
USERNAME	
PASSWORD	
NOTE	

WEBSITE	
USERNAME	
PASSWORD	
NOTE	

WEBSITE	
USERNAME	
PASSWORD	
NOTE	

WEBSITE	
USERNAME	
PASSWORD	
NOTE	

WEBSITE	
USERNAME	
PASSWORD	
NOTE	

WEBSITE	
USERNAME	
PASSWORD	
NOTE	

WEBSITE	
USERNAME	
PASSWORD	
NOTE	

WEBSITE	
USERNAME	
PASSWORD	
NOTE	

WEBSITE	
USERNAME	
PASSWORD	
NOTE	

WEBSITE	
USERNAME	
PASSWORD	
NOTE	

WEBSITE	
USERNAME	
PASSWORD	
NOTE	

WEBSITE	
USERNAME	
PASSWORD	
NOTE	

WEBSITE	
USERNAME	
PASSWORD	
NOTE	

WEBSITE	
USERNAME	
PASSWORD	
NOTE	

WEBSITE	
USERNAME	
PASSWORD	
NOTE	

C

WEBSITE	
USERNAME	
PASSWORD	
NOTE	

WEBSITE	
USERNAME	
PASSWORD	
NOTE	

WEBSITE	
USERNAME	
PASSWORD	
NOTE	

WEBSITE	
USERNAME	
PASSWORD	
NOTE	

WEBSITE	
USERNAME	
PASSWORD	
NOTE	

WEBSITE	
USERNAME	
PASSWORD	
NOTE	

WEBSITE	
USERNAME	
PASSWORD	
NOTE	

WEBSITE	
USERNAME	
PASSWORD	
NOTE	

WEBSITE	
USERNAME	
PASSWORD	
NOTE	

WEBSITE	
USERNAME	
PASSWORD	
NOTE	

C

WEBSITE	
USERNAME	
PASSWORD	
NOTE	

WEBSITE	
USERNAME	
PASSWORD	
NOTE	

WEBSITE	
USERNAME	
PASSWORD	
NOTE	

WEBSITE	
USERNAME	
PASSWORD	
NOTE	

WEBSITE	
USERNAME	
PASSWORD	
NOTE	

<table>
<tr><td>WEBSITE</td><td></td></tr>
<tr><td>USERNAME</td><td></td></tr>
<tr><td>PASSWORD</td><td></td></tr>
<tr><td>NOTE</td><td></td></tr>
</table>

<table>
<tr><td>WEBSITE</td><td></td></tr>
<tr><td>USERNAME</td><td></td></tr>
<tr><td>PASSWORD</td><td></td></tr>
<tr><td>NOTE</td><td></td></tr>
</table>

<table>
<tr><td>WEBSITE</td><td></td></tr>
<tr><td>USERNAME</td><td></td></tr>
<tr><td>PASSWORD</td><td></td></tr>
<tr><td>NOTE</td><td></td></tr>
</table>

<table>
<tr><td>WEBSITE</td><td></td></tr>
<tr><td>USERNAME</td><td></td></tr>
<tr><td>PASSWORD</td><td></td></tr>
<tr><td>NOTE</td><td></td></tr>
</table>

<table>
<tr><td>WEBSITE</td><td></td></tr>
<tr><td>USERNAME</td><td></td></tr>
<tr><td>PASSWORD</td><td></td></tr>
<tr><td>NOTE</td><td></td></tr>
</table>

D

WEBSITE	
USERNAME	
PASSWORD	
NOTE	

WEBSITE	
USERNAME	
PASSWORD	
NOTE	

WEBSITE	
USERNAME	
PASSWORD	
NOTE	

WEBSITE	
USERNAME	
PASSWORD	
NOTE	

WEBSITE	
USERNAME	
PASSWORD	
NOTE	

D

WEBSITE	
USERNAME	
PASSWORD	
NOTE	

WEBSITE	
USERNAME	
PASSWORD	
NOTE	

WEBSITE	
USERNAME	
PASSWORD	
NOTE	

WEBSITE	
USERNAME	
PASSWORD	
NOTE	

WEBSITE	
USERNAME	
PASSWORD	
NOTE	

WEBSITE	
USERNAME	
PASSWORD	
NOTE	

WEBSITE	
USERNAME	
PASSWORD	
NOTE	

WEBSITE	
USERNAME	
PASSWORD	
NOTE	

WEBSITE	
USERNAME	
PASSWORD	
NOTE	

WEBSITE	
USERNAME	
PASSWORD	
NOTE	

WEBSITE	
USERNAME	
PASSWORD	
NOTE	

WEBSITE	
USERNAME	
PASSWORD	
NOTE	

WEBSITE	
USERNAME	
PASSWORD	
NOTE	

WEBSITE	
USERNAME	
PASSWORD	
NOTE	

WEBSITE	
USERNAME	
PASSWORD	
NOTE	

<table>
<tr><td>E</td><td></td></tr>
</table>

WEBSITE	
USERNAME	
PASSWORD	
NOTE	

WEBSITE	
USERNAME	
PASSWORD	
NOTE	

WEBSITE	
USERNAME	
PASSWORD	
NOTE	

WEBSITE	
USERNAME	
PASSWORD	
NOTE	

WEBSITE	
USERNAME	
PASSWORD	
NOTE	

WEBSITE	
USERNAME	
PASSWORD	
NOTE	

WEBSITE	
USERNAME	
PASSWORD	
NOTE	

WEBSITE	
USERNAME	
PASSWORD	
NOTE	

WEBSITE	
USERNAME	
PASSWORD	
NOTE	

WEBSITE	
USERNAME	
PASSWORD	
NOTE	

WEBSITE	
USERNAME	
PASSWORD	
NOTE	

WEBSITE	
USERNAME	
PASSWORD	
NOTE	

WEBSITE	
USERNAME	
PASSWORD	
NOTE	

WEBSITE	
USERNAME	
PASSWORD	
NOTE	

WEBSITE	
USERNAME	
PASSWORD	
NOTE	

WEBSITE	
USERNAME	
PASSWORD	
NOTE	

WEBSITE	
USERNAME	
PASSWORD	
NOTE	

WEBSITE	
USERNAME	
PASSWORD	
NOTE	

WEBSITE	
USERNAME	
PASSWORD	
NOTE	

WEBSITE	
USERNAME	
PASSWORD	
NOTE	

WEBSITE	
USERNAME	
PASSWORD	
NOTE	

WEBSITE	
USERNAME	
PASSWORD	
NOTE	

WEBSITE	
USERNAME	
PASSWORD	
NOTE	

WEBSITE	
USERNAME	
PASSWORD	
NOTE	

WEBSITE	
USERNAME	
PASSWORD	
NOTE	

F

WEBSITE	
USERNAME	
PASSWORD	
NOTE	

WEBSITE	
USERNAME	
PASSWORD	
NOTE	

WEBSITE	
USERNAME	
PASSWORD	
NOTE	

WEBSITE	
USERNAME	
PASSWORD	
NOTE	

WEBSITE	
USERNAME	
PASSWORD	
NOTE	

F

WEBSITE	
USERNAME	
PASSWORD	
NOTE	

WEBSITE	
USERNAME	
PASSWORD	
NOTE	

WEBSITE	
USERNAME	
PASSWORD	
NOTE	

WEBSITE	
USERNAME	
PASSWORD	
NOTE	

WEBSITE	
USERNAME	
PASSWORD	
NOTE	

WEBSITE	
USERNAME	
PASSWORD	
NOTE	

WEBSITE	
USERNAME	
PASSWORD	
NOTE	

WEBSITE	
USERNAME	
PASSWORD	
NOTE	

WEBSITE	
USERNAME	
PASSWORD	
NOTE	

WEBSITE	
USERNAME	
PASSWORD	
NOTE	

<table>
<tr><td>**G**</td><td></td></tr>
<tr><td>WEBSITE</td><td></td></tr>
<tr><td>USERNAME</td><td></td></tr>
<tr><td>PASSWORD</td><td></td></tr>
<tr><td>NOTE</td><td></td></tr>
</table>

WEBSITE	
USERNAME	
PASSWORD	
NOTE	

WEBSITE	
USERNAME	
PASSWORD	
NOTE	

WEBSITE	
USERNAME	
PASSWORD	
NOTE	

WEBSITE	
USERNAME	
PASSWORD	
NOTE	

WEBSITE	
USERNAME	
PASSWORD	
NOTE	

WEBSITE	
USERNAME	
PASSWORD	
NOTE	

WEBSITE	
USERNAME	
PASSWORD	
NOTE	

WEBSITE	
USERNAME	
PASSWORD	
NOTE	

WEBSITE	
USERNAME	
PASSWORD	
NOTE	

G

WEBSITE	
USERNAME	
PASSWORD	
NOTE	

WEBSITE	
USERNAME	
PASSWORD	
NOTE	

WEBSITE	
USERNAME	
PASSWORD	
NOTE	

WEBSITE	
USERNAME	
PASSWORD	
NOTE	

WEBSITE	
USERNAME	
PASSWORD	
NOTE	

WEBSITE	
USERNAME	
PASSWORD	
NOTE	

WEBSITE	
USERNAME	
PASSWORD	
NOTE	

WEBSITE	
USERNAME	
PASSWORD	
NOTE	

WEBSITE	
USERNAME	
PASSWORD	
NOTE	

WEBSITE	
USERNAME	
PASSWORD	
NOTE	

WEBSITE	
USERNAME	
PASSWORD	
NOTE	

WEBSITE	
USERNAME	
PASSWORD	
NOTE	

WEBSITE	
USERNAME	
PASSWORD	
NOTE	

WEBSITE	
USERNAME	
PASSWORD	
NOTE	

WEBSITE	
USERNAME	
PASSWORD	
NOTE	

WEBSITE	
USERNAME	
PASSWORD	
NOTE	

WEBSITE	
USERNAME	
PASSWORD	
NOTE	

WEBSITE	
USERNAME	
PASSWORD	
NOTE	

WEBSITE	
USERNAME	
PASSWORD	
NOTE	

WEBSITE	
USERNAME	
PASSWORD	
NOTE	

<table>
<tr><td>H</td></tr>
</table>

WEBSITE	
USERNAME	
PASSWORD	
NOTE	

WEBSITE	
USERNAME	
PASSWORD	
NOTE	

WEBSITE	
USERNAME	
PASSWORD	
NOTE	

WEBSITE	
USERNAME	
PASSWORD	
NOTE	

WEBSITE	
USERNAME	
PASSWORD	
NOTE	

WEBSITE	
USERNAME	
PASSWORD	
NOTE	

WEBSITE	
USERNAME	
PASSWORD	
NOTE	

WEBSITE	
USERNAME	
PASSWORD	
NOTE	

WEBSITE	
USERNAME	
PASSWORD	
NOTE	

WEBSITE	
USERNAME	
PASSWORD	
NOTE	

I

WEBSITE	
USERNAME	
PASSWORD	
NOTE	

WEBSITE	
USERNAME	
PASSWORD	
NOTE	

WEBSITE	
USERNAME	
PASSWORD	
NOTE	

WEBSITE	
USERNAME	
PASSWORD	
NOTE	

WEBSITE	
USERNAME	
PASSWORD	
NOTE	

WEBSITE	
USERNAME	
PASSWORD	
NOTE	

WEBSITE	
USERNAME	
PASSWORD	
NOTE	

WEBSITE	
USERNAME	
PASSWORD	
NOTE	

WEBSITE	
USERNAME	
PASSWORD	
NOTE	

WEBSITE	
USERNAME	
PASSWORD	
NOTE	

I	
WEBSITE	
USERNAME	
PASSWORD	
NOTE	

WEBSITE	
USERNAME	
PASSWORD	
NOTE	

WEBSITE	
USERNAME	
PASSWORD	
NOTE	

WEBSITE	
USERNAME	
PASSWORD	
NOTE	

WEBSITE	
USERNAME	
PASSWORD	
NOTE	

WEBSITE	
USERNAME	
PASSWORD	
NOTE	

WEBSITE	
USERNAME	
PASSWORD	
NOTE	

WEBSITE	
USERNAME	
PASSWORD	
NOTE	

WEBSITE	
USERNAME	
PASSWORD	
NOTE	

WEBSITE	
USERNAME	
PASSWORD	
NOTE	

J

WEBSITE	
USERNAME	
PASSWORD	
NOTE	

WEBSITE	
USERNAME	
PASSWORD	
NOTE	

WEBSITE	
USERNAME	
PASSWORD	
NOTE	

WEBSITE	
USERNAME	
PASSWORD	
NOTE	

WEBSITE	
USERNAME	
PASSWORD	
NOTE	

WEBSITE	
USERNAME	
PASSWORD	
NOTE	

WEBSITE	
USERNAME	
PASSWORD	
NOTE	

WEBSITE	
USERNAME	
PASSWORD	
NOTE	

WEBSITE	
USERNAME	
PASSWORD	
NOTE	

WEBSITE	
USERNAME	
PASSWORD	
NOTE	

<table>
<tr><td>J</td><td></td></tr>
</table>

WEBSITE	
USERNAME	
PASSWORD	
NOTE	

WEBSITE	
USERNAME	
PASSWORD	
NOTE	

WEBSITE	
USERNAME	
PASSWORD	
NOTE	

WEBSITE	
USERNAME	
PASSWORD	
NOTE	

WEBSITE	
USERNAME	
PASSWORD	
NOTE	

WEBSITE	
USERNAME	
PASSWORD	
NOTE	

WEBSITE	
USERNAME	
PASSWORD	
NOTE	

WEBSITE	
USERNAME	
PASSWORD	
NOTE	

WEBSITE	
USERNAME	
PASSWORD	
NOTE	

WEBSITE	
USERNAME	
PASSWORD	
NOTE	

<table>
<tr><td colspan="2">K</td></tr>
<tr><td>WEBSITE</td><td></td></tr>
<tr><td>USERNAME</td><td></td></tr>
<tr><td>PASSWORD</td><td></td></tr>
<tr><td>NOTE</td><td></td></tr>
</table>

<table>
<tr><td>WEBSITE</td><td></td></tr>
<tr><td>USERNAME</td><td></td></tr>
<tr><td>PASSWORD</td><td></td></tr>
<tr><td>NOTE</td><td></td></tr>
</table>

<table>
<tr><td>WEBSITE</td><td></td></tr>
<tr><td>USERNAME</td><td></td></tr>
<tr><td>PASSWORD</td><td></td></tr>
<tr><td>NOTE</td><td></td></tr>
</table>

<table>
<tr><td>WEBSITE</td><td></td></tr>
<tr><td>USERNAME</td><td></td></tr>
<tr><td>PASSWORD</td><td></td></tr>
<tr><td>NOTE</td><td></td></tr>
</table>

<table>
<tr><td>WEBSITE</td><td></td></tr>
<tr><td>USERNAME</td><td></td></tr>
<tr><td>PASSWORD</td><td></td></tr>
<tr><td>NOTE</td><td></td></tr>
</table>

WEBSITE	
USERNAME	
PASSWORD	
NOTE	

WEBSITE	
USERNAME	
PASSWORD	
NOTE	

WEBSITE	
USERNAME	
PASSWORD	
NOTE	

WEBSITE	
USERNAME	
PASSWORD	
NOTE	

WEBSITE	
USERNAME	
PASSWORD	
NOTE	

K

WEBSITE	
USERNAME	
PASSWORD	
NOTE	

WEBSITE	
USERNAME	
PASSWORD	
NOTE	

WEBSITE	
USERNAME	
PASSWORD	
NOTE	

WEBSITE	
USERNAME	
PASSWORD	
NOTE	

WEBSITE	
USERNAME	
PASSWORD	
NOTE	

WEBSITE	
USERNAME	
PASSWORD	
NOTE	

WEBSITE	
USERNAME	
PASSWORD	
NOTE	

WEBSITE	
USERNAME	
PASSWORD	
NOTE	

WEBSITE	
USERNAME	
PASSWORD	
NOTE	

WEBSITE	
USERNAME	
PASSWORD	
NOTE	

WEBSITE	
USERNAME	
PASSWORD	
NOTE	

WEBSITE	
USERNAME	
PASSWORD	
NOTE	

WEBSITE	
USERNAME	
PASSWORD	
NOTE	

WEBSITE	
USERNAME	
PASSWORD	
NOTE	

WEBSITE	
USERNAME	
PASSWORD	
NOTE	

L

WEBSITE	
USERNAME	
PASSWORD	
NOTE	

WEBSITE	
USERNAME	
PASSWORD	
NOTE	

WEBSITE	
USERNAME	
PASSWORD	
NOTE	

WEBSITE	
USERNAME	
PASSWORD	
NOTE	

WEBSITE	
USERNAME	
PASSWORD	
NOTE	

L

WEBSITE	
USERNAME	
PASSWORD	
NOTE	

WEBSITE	
USERNAME	
PASSWORD	
NOTE	

WEBSITE	
USERNAME	
PASSWORD	
NOTE	

WEBSITE	
USERNAME	
PASSWORD	
NOTE	

WEBSITE	
USERNAME	
PASSWORD	
NOTE	

<table>
<tr><td>**L**</td></tr>
</table>

WEBSITE	
USERNAME	
PASSWORD	
NOTE	

WEBSITE	
USERNAME	
PASSWORD	
NOTE	

WEBSITE	
USERNAME	
PASSWORD	
NOTE	

WEBSITE	
USERNAME	
PASSWORD	
NOTE	

WEBSITE	
USERNAME	
PASSWORD	
NOTE	

M

WEBSITE	
USERNAME	
PASSWORD	
NOTE	

WEBSITE	
USERNAME	
PASSWORD	
NOTE	

WEBSITE	
USERNAME	
PASSWORD	
NOTE	

WEBSITE	
USERNAME	
PASSWORD	
NOTE	

WEBSITE	
USERNAME	
PASSWORD	
NOTE	

WEBSITE	
USERNAME	
PASSWORD	
NOTE	

WEBSITE	
USERNAME	
PASSWORD	
NOTE	

WEBSITE	
USERNAME	
PASSWORD	
NOTE	

WEBSITE	
USERNAME	
PASSWORD	
NOTE	

WEBSITE	
USERNAME	
PASSWORD	
NOTE	

M

WEBSITE	
USERNAME	
PASSWORD	
NOTE	

WEBSITE	
USERNAME	
PASSWORD	
NOTE	

WEBSITE	
USERNAME	
PASSWORD	
NOTE	

WEBSITE	
USERNAME	
PASSWORD	
NOTE	

WEBSITE	
USERNAME	
PASSWORD	
NOTE	

WEBSITE	
USERNAME	
PASSWORD	
NOTE	

WEBSITE	
USERNAME	
PASSWORD	
NOTE	

WEBSITE	
USERNAME	
PASSWORD	
NOTE	

WEBSITE	
USERNAME	
PASSWORD	
NOTE	

WEBSITE	
USERNAME	
PASSWORD	
NOTE	

<table>
<tr><td>N</td><td></td></tr>
</table>

WEBSITE	
USERNAME	
PASSWORD	
NOTE	

WEBSITE	
USERNAME	
PASSWORD	
NOTE	

WEBSITE	
USERNAME	
PASSWORD	
NOTE	

WEBSITE	
USERNAME	
PASSWORD	
NOTE	

WEBSITE	
USERNAME	
PASSWORD	
NOTE	

WEBSITE	
USERNAME	
PASSWORD	
NOTE	

WEBSITE	
USERNAME	
PASSWORD	
NOTE	

WEBSITE	
USERNAME	
PASSWORD	
NOTE	

WEBSITE	
USERNAME	
PASSWORD	
NOTE	

WEBSITE	
USERNAME	
PASSWORD	
NOTE	

WEBSITE	
USERNAME	
PASSWORD	
NOTE	

WEBSITE	
USERNAME	
PASSWORD	
NOTE	

WEBSITE	
USERNAME	
PASSWORD	
NOTE	

WEBSITE	
USERNAME	
PASSWORD	
NOTE	

WEBSITE	
USERNAME	
PASSWORD	
NOTE	

WEBSITE	
USERNAME	
PASSWORD	
NOTE	

WEBSITE	
USERNAME	
PASSWORD	
NOTE	

WEBSITE	
USERNAME	
PASSWORD	
NOTE	

WEBSITE	
USERNAME	
PASSWORD	
NOTE	

WEBSITE	
USERNAME	
PASSWORD	
NOTE	

WEBSITE	
USERNAME	
PASSWORD	
NOTE	

WEBSITE	
USERNAME	
PASSWORD	
NOTE	

WEBSITE	
USERNAME	
PASSWORD	
NOTE	

WEBSITE	
USERNAME	
PASSWORD	
NOTE	

WEBSITE	
USERNAME	
PASSWORD	
NOTE	

WEBSITE	
USERNAME	
PASSWORD	
NOTE	

WEBSITE	
USERNAME	
PASSWORD	
NOTE	

WEBSITE	
USERNAME	
PASSWORD	
NOTE	

WEBSITE	
USERNAME	
PASSWORD	
NOTE	

WEBSITE	
USERNAME	
PASSWORD	
NOTE	

WEBSITE	
USERNAME	
PASSWORD	
NOTE	

WEBSITE	
USERNAME	
PASSWORD	
NOTE	

WEBSITE	
USERNAME	
PASSWORD	
NOTE	

WEBSITE	
USERNAME	
PASSWORD	
NOTE	

WEBSITE	
USERNAME	
PASSWORD	
NOTE	

WEBSITE	
USERNAME	
PASSWORD	
NOTE	

WEBSITE	
USERNAME	
PASSWORD	
NOTE	

WEBSITE	
USERNAME	
PASSWORD	
NOTE	

WEBSITE	
USERNAME	
PASSWORD	
NOTE	

WEBSITE	
USERNAME	
PASSWORD	
NOTE	

WEBSITE	
USERNAME	
PASSWORD	
NOTE	

WEBSITE	
USERNAME	
PASSWORD	
NOTE	

WEBSITE	
USERNAME	
PASSWORD	
NOTE	

WEBSITE	
USERNAME	
PASSWORD	
NOTE	

WEBSITE	
USERNAME	
PASSWORD	
NOTE	

WEBSITE	
USERNAME	
PASSWORD	
NOTE	

WEBSITE	
USERNAME	
PASSWORD	
NOTE	

WEBSITE	
USERNAME	
PASSWORD	
NOTE	

WEBSITE	
USERNAME	
PASSWORD	
NOTE	

WEBSITE	
USERNAME	
PASSWORD	
NOTE	

P

WEBSITE	
USERNAME	
PASSWORD	
NOTE	

WEBSITE	
USERNAME	
PASSWORD	
NOTE	

WEBSITE	
USERNAME	
PASSWORD	
NOTE	

WEBSITE	
USERNAME	
PASSWORD	
NOTE	

WEBSITE	
USERNAME	
PASSWORD	
NOTE	

<table>
<tr><td>WEBSITE</td><td></td></tr>
<tr><td>USERNAME</td><td></td></tr>
<tr><td>PASSWORD</td><td></td></tr>
<tr><td>NOTE</td><td></td></tr>
</table>

<table>
<tr><td>WEBSITE</td><td></td></tr>
<tr><td>USERNAME</td><td></td></tr>
<tr><td>PASSWORD</td><td></td></tr>
<tr><td>NOTE</td><td></td></tr>
</table>

<table>
<tr><td>WEBSITE</td><td></td></tr>
<tr><td>USERNAME</td><td></td></tr>
<tr><td>PASSWORD</td><td></td></tr>
<tr><td>NOTE</td><td></td></tr>
</table>

<table>
<tr><td>WEBSITE</td><td></td></tr>
<tr><td>USERNAME</td><td></td></tr>
<tr><td>PASSWORD</td><td></td></tr>
<tr><td>NOTE</td><td></td></tr>
</table>

<table>
<tr><td>WEBSITE</td><td></td></tr>
<tr><td>USERNAME</td><td></td></tr>
<tr><td>PASSWORD</td><td></td></tr>
<tr><td>NOTE</td><td></td></tr>
</table>

WEBSITE	
USERNAME	
PASSWORD	
NOTE	

WEBSITE	
USERNAME	
PASSWORD	
NOTE	

WEBSITE	
USERNAME	
PASSWORD	
NOTE	

WEBSITE	
USERNAME	
PASSWORD	
NOTE	

WEBSITE	
USERNAME	
PASSWORD	
NOTE	

WEBSITE	
USERNAME	
PASSWORD	
NOTE	

WEBSITE	
USERNAME	
PASSWORD	
NOTE	

WEBSITE	
USERNAME	
PASSWORD	
NOTE	

WEBSITE	
USERNAME	
PASSWORD	
NOTE	

WEBSITE	
USERNAME	
PASSWORD	
NOTE	

WEBSITE	
USERNAME	
PASSWORD	
NOTE	

WEBSITE	
USERNAME	
PASSWORD	
NOTE	

WEBSITE	
USERNAME	
PASSWORD	
NOTE	

WEBSITE	
USERNAME	
PASSWORD	
NOTE	

WEBSITE	
USERNAME	
PASSWORD	
NOTE	

WEBSITE	
USERNAME	
PASSWORD	
NOTE	

WEBSITE	
USERNAME	
PASSWORD	
NOTE	

WEBSITE	
USERNAME	
PASSWORD	
NOTE	

WEBSITE	
USERNAME	
PASSWORD	
NOTE	

WEBSITE	
USERNAME	
PASSWORD	
NOTE	

R

WEBSITE	
USERNAME	
PASSWORD	
NOTE	

WEBSITE	
USERNAME	
PASSWORD	
NOTE	

WEBSITE	
USERNAME	
PASSWORD	
NOTE	

WEBSITE	
USERNAME	
PASSWORD	
NOTE	

WEBSITE	
USERNAME	
PASSWORD	
NOTE	

R

WEBSITE	
USERNAME	
PASSWORD	
NOTE	

WEBSITE	
USERNAME	
PASSWORD	
NOTE	

WEBSITE	
USERNAME	
PASSWORD	
NOTE	

WEBSITE	
USERNAME	
PASSWORD	
NOTE	

WEBSITE	
USERNAME	
PASSWORD	
NOTE	

R

WEBSITE	
USERNAME	
PASSWORD	
NOTE	

WEBSITE	
USERNAME	
PASSWORD	
NOTE	

WEBSITE	
USERNAME	
PASSWORD	
NOTE	

WEBSITE	
USERNAME	
PASSWORD	
NOTE	

WEBSITE	
USERNAME	
PASSWORD	
NOTE	

R

WEBSITE	
USERNAME	
PASSWORD	
NOTE	

WEBSITE	
USERNAME	
PASSWORD	
NOTE	

WEBSITE	
USERNAME	
PASSWORD	
NOTE	

WEBSITE	
USERNAME	
PASSWORD	
NOTE	

WEBSITE	
USERNAME	
PASSWORD	
NOTE	

S

WEBSITE	
USERNAME	
PASSWORD	
NOTE	

WEBSITE	
USERNAME	
PASSWORD	
NOTE	

WEBSITE	
USERNAME	
PASSWORD	
NOTE	

WEBSITE	
USERNAME	
PASSWORD	
NOTE	

WEBSITE	
USERNAME	
PASSWORD	
NOTE	

S

WEBSITE	
USERNAME	
PASSWORD	
NOTE	

WEBSITE	
USERNAME	
PASSWORD	
NOTE	

WEBSITE	
USERNAME	
PASSWORD	
NOTE	

WEBSITE	
USERNAME	
PASSWORD	
NOTE	

WEBSITE	
USERNAME	
PASSWORD	
NOTE	

WEBSITE	
USERNAME	
PASSWORD	
NOTE	

WEBSITE	
USERNAME	
PASSWORD	
NOTE	

WEBSITE	
USERNAME	
PASSWORD	
NOTE	

WEBSITE	
USERNAME	
PASSWORD	
NOTE	

WEBSITE	
USERNAME	
PASSWORD	
NOTE	

WEBSITE	
USERNAME	
PASSWORD	
NOTE	

WEBSITE	
USERNAME	
PASSWORD	
NOTE	

WEBSITE	
USERNAME	
PASSWORD	
NOTE	

WEBSITE	
USERNAME	
PASSWORD	
NOTE	

WEBSITE	
USERNAME	
PASSWORD	
NOTE	

WEBSITE	
USERNAME	
PASSWORD	
NOTE	

WEBSITE	
USERNAME	
PASSWORD	
NOTE	

WEBSITE	
USERNAME	
PASSWORD	
NOTE	

WEBSITE	
USERNAME	
PASSWORD	
NOTE	

WEBSITE	
USERNAME	
PASSWORD	
NOTE	

T

WEBSITE	
USERNAME	
PASSWORD	
NOTE	

WEBSITE	
USERNAME	
PASSWORD	
NOTE	

WEBSITE	
USERNAME	
PASSWORD	
NOTE	

WEBSITE	
USERNAME	
PASSWORD	
NOTE	

WEBSITE	
USERNAME	
PASSWORD	
NOTE	

T

WEBSITE	
USERNAME	
PASSWORD	
NOTE	

WEBSITE	
USERNAME	
PASSWORD	
NOTE	

WEBSITE	
USERNAME	
PASSWORD	
NOTE	

WEBSITE	
USERNAME	
PASSWORD	
NOTE	

WEBSITE	
USERNAME	
PASSWORD	
NOTE	

T

WEBSITE	
USERNAME	
PASSWORD	
NOTE	

WEBSITE	
USERNAME	
PASSWORD	
NOTE	

WEBSITE	
USERNAME	
PASSWORD	
NOTE	

WEBSITE	
USERNAME	
PASSWORD	
NOTE	

WEBSITE	
USERNAME	
PASSWORD	
NOTE	

WEBSITE	
USERNAME	
PASSWORD	
NOTE	

WEBSITE	
USERNAME	
PASSWORD	
NOTE	

WEBSITE	
USERNAME	
PASSWORD	
NOTE	

WEBSITE	
USERNAME	
PASSWORD	
NOTE	

WEBSITE	
USERNAME	
PASSWORD	
NOTE	

U

WEBSITE	
USERNAME	
PASSWORD	
NOTE	

WEBSITE	
USERNAME	
PASSWORD	
NOTE	

WEBSITE	
USERNAME	
PASSWORD	
NOTE	

WEBSITE	
USERNAME	
PASSWORD	
NOTE	

WEBSITE	
USERNAME	
PASSWORD	
NOTE	

WEBSITE	
USERNAME	
PASSWORD	
NOTE	

WEBSITE	
USERNAME	
PASSWORD	
NOTE	

WEBSITE	
USERNAME	
PASSWORD	
NOTE	

WEBSITE	
USERNAME	
PASSWORD	
NOTE	

WEBSITE	
USERNAME	
PASSWORD	
NOTE	

WEBSITE	
USERNAME	
PASSWORD	
NOTE	

WEBSITE	
USERNAME	
PASSWORD	
NOTE	

WEBSITE	
USERNAME	
PASSWORD	
NOTE	

WEBSITE	
USERNAME	
PASSWORD	
NOTE	

WEBSITE	
USERNAME	
PASSWORD	
NOTE	

WEBSITE	
USERNAME	
PASSWORD	
NOTE	

WEBSITE	
USERNAME	
PASSWORD	
NOTE	

WEBSITE	
USERNAME	
PASSWORD	
NOTE	

WEBSITE	
USERNAME	
PASSWORD	
NOTE	

WEBSITE	
USERNAME	
PASSWORD	
NOTE	

WEBSITE	
USERNAME	
PASSWORD	
NOTE	

WEBSITE	
USERNAME	
PASSWORD	
NOTE	

WEBSITE	
USERNAME	
PASSWORD	
NOTE	

WEBSITE	
USERNAME	
PASSWORD	
NOTE	

WEBSITE	
USERNAME	
PASSWORD	
NOTE	

V

WEBSITE	
USERNAME	
PASSWORD	
NOTE	

WEBSITE	
USERNAME	
PASSWORD	
NOTE	

WEBSITE	
USERNAME	
PASSWORD	
NOTE	

WEBSITE	
USERNAME	
PASSWORD	
NOTE	

WEBSITE	
USERNAME	
PASSWORD	
NOTE	

V

WEBSITE	
USERNAME	
PASSWORD	
NOTE	

WEBSITE	
USERNAME	
PASSWORD	
NOTE	

WEBSITE	
USERNAME	
PASSWORD	
NOTE	

WEBSITE	
USERNAME	
PASSWORD	
NOTE	

WEBSITE	
USERNAME	
PASSWORD	
NOTE	

<table>
<tr><td colspan="2">W</td></tr>
<tr><td>WEBSITE</td><td></td></tr>
<tr><td>USERNAME</td><td></td></tr>
<tr><td>PASSWORD</td><td></td></tr>
<tr><td>NOTE</td><td></td></tr>
</table>

<table>
<tr><td>WEBSITE</td><td></td></tr>
<tr><td>USERNAME</td><td></td></tr>
<tr><td>PASSWORD</td><td></td></tr>
<tr><td>NOTE</td><td></td></tr>
</table>

<table>
<tr><td>WEBSITE</td><td></td></tr>
<tr><td>USERNAME</td><td></td></tr>
<tr><td>PASSWORD</td><td></td></tr>
<tr><td>NOTE</td><td></td></tr>
</table>

<table>
<tr><td>WEBSITE</td><td></td></tr>
<tr><td>USERNAME</td><td></td></tr>
<tr><td>PASSWORD</td><td></td></tr>
<tr><td>NOTE</td><td></td></tr>
</table>

<table>
<tr><td>WEBSITE</td><td></td></tr>
<tr><td>USERNAME</td><td></td></tr>
<tr><td>PASSWORD</td><td></td></tr>
<tr><td>NOTE</td><td></td></tr>
</table>

WEBSITE	
USERNAME	
PASSWORD	
NOTE	

WEBSITE	
USERNAME	
PASSWORD	
NOTE	

WEBSITE	
USERNAME	
PASSWORD	
NOTE	

WEBSITE	
USERNAME	
PASSWORD	
NOTE	

WEBSITE	
USERNAME	
PASSWORD	
NOTE	

<table>
<tr><td>**W**</td><td></td></tr>
</table>

WEBSITE	
USERNAME	
PASSWORD	
NOTE	

WEBSITE	
USERNAME	
PASSWORD	
NOTE	

WEBSITE	
USERNAME	
PASSWORD	
NOTE	

WEBSITE	
USERNAME	
PASSWORD	
NOTE	

WEBSITE	
USERNAME	
PASSWORD	
NOTE	

W

WEBSITE	
USERNAME	
PASSWORD	
NOTE	

WEBSITE	
USERNAME	
PASSWORD	
NOTE	

WEBSITE	
USERNAME	
PASSWORD	
NOTE	

WEBSITE	
USERNAME	
PASSWORD	
NOTE	

WEBSITE	
USERNAME	
PASSWORD	
NOTE	

X

WEBSITE	
USERNAME	
PASSWORD	
NOTE	

WEBSITE	
USERNAME	
PASSWORD	
NOTE	

WEBSITE	
USERNAME	
PASSWORD	
NOTE	

WEBSITE	
USERNAME	
PASSWORD	
NOTE	

WEBSITE	
USERNAME	
PASSWORD	
NOTE	

WEBSITE	
USERNAME	
PASSWORD	
NOTE	

WEBSITE	
USERNAME	
PASSWORD	
NOTE	

WEBSITE	
USERNAME	
PASSWORD	
NOTE	

WEBSITE	
USERNAME	
PASSWORD	
NOTE	

WEBSITE	
USERNAME	
PASSWORD	
NOTE	

<table>
<tr><td>X</td><td></td></tr>
<tr><td>WEBSITE</td><td></td></tr>
<tr><td>USERNAME</td><td></td></tr>
<tr><td>PASSWORD</td><td></td></tr>
<tr><td>NOTE</td><td></td></tr>
</table>

<table>
<tr><td>WEBSITE</td><td></td></tr>
<tr><td>USERNAME</td><td></td></tr>
<tr><td>PASSWORD</td><td></td></tr>
<tr><td>NOTE</td><td></td></tr>
</table>

<table>
<tr><td>WEBSITE</td><td></td></tr>
<tr><td>USERNAME</td><td></td></tr>
<tr><td>PASSWORD</td><td></td></tr>
<tr><td>NOTE</td><td></td></tr>
</table>

<table>
<tr><td>WEBSITE</td><td></td></tr>
<tr><td>USERNAME</td><td></td></tr>
<tr><td>PASSWORD</td><td></td></tr>
<tr><td>NOTE</td><td></td></tr>
</table>

<table>
<tr><td>WEBSITE</td><td></td></tr>
<tr><td>USERNAME</td><td></td></tr>
<tr><td>PASSWORD</td><td></td></tr>
<tr><td>NOTE</td><td></td></tr>
</table>

WEBSITE	
USERNAME	
PASSWORD	
NOTE	

WEBSITE	
USERNAME	
PASSWORD	
NOTE	

WEBSITE	
USERNAME	
PASSWORD	
NOTE	

WEBSITE	
USERNAME	
PASSWORD	
NOTE	

WEBSITE	
USERNAME	
PASSWORD	
NOTE	

WEBSITE	
USERNAME	
PASSWORD	
NOTE	

WEBSITE	
USERNAME	
PASSWORD	
NOTE	

WEBSITE	
USERNAME	
PASSWORD	
NOTE	

WEBSITE	
USERNAME	
PASSWORD	
NOTE	

WEBSITE	
USERNAME	
PASSWORD	
NOTE	

WEBSITE	
USERNAME	
PASSWORD	
NOTE	

WEBSITE	
USERNAME	
PASSWORD	
NOTE	

WEBSITE	
USERNAME	
PASSWORD	
NOTE	

WEBSITE	
USERNAME	
PASSWORD	
NOTE	

WEBSITE	
USERNAME	
PASSWORD	
NOTE	

WEBSITE	
USERNAME	
PASSWORD	
NOTE	

WEBSITE	
USERNAME	
PASSWORD	
NOTE	

WEBSITE	
USERNAME	
PASSWORD	
NOTE	

WEBSITE	
USERNAME	
PASSWORD	
NOTE	

WEBSITE	
USERNAME	
PASSWORD	
NOTE	

<table>
<tr><td>WEBSITE</td><td></td></tr>
<tr><td>USERNAME</td><td></td></tr>
<tr><td>PASSWORD</td><td></td></tr>
<tr><td>NOTE</td><td></td></tr>
</table>

<table>
<tr><td>WEBSITE</td><td></td></tr>
<tr><td>USERNAME</td><td></td></tr>
<tr><td>PASSWORD</td><td></td></tr>
<tr><td>NOTE</td><td></td></tr>
</table>

<table>
<tr><td>WEBSITE</td><td></td></tr>
<tr><td>USERNAME</td><td></td></tr>
<tr><td>PASSWORD</td><td></td></tr>
<tr><td>NOTE</td><td></td></tr>
</table>

<table>
<tr><td>WEBSITE</td><td></td></tr>
<tr><td>USERNAME</td><td></td></tr>
<tr><td>PASSWORD</td><td></td></tr>
<tr><td>NOTE</td><td></td></tr>
</table>

<table>
<tr><td>WEBSITE</td><td></td></tr>
<tr><td>USERNAME</td><td></td></tr>
<tr><td>PASSWORD</td><td></td></tr>
<tr><td>NOTE</td><td></td></tr>
</table>

Z

WEBSITE	
USERNAME	
PASSWORD	
NOTE	

WEBSITE	
USERNAME	
PASSWORD	
NOTE	

WEBSITE	
USERNAME	
PASSWORD	
NOTE	

WEBSITE	
USERNAME	
PASSWORD	
NOTE	

WEBSITE	
USERNAME	
PASSWORD	
NOTE	

WEBSITE	
USERNAME	
PASSWORD	
NOTE	

WEBSITE	
USERNAME	
PASSWORD	
NOTE	

WEBSITE	
USERNAME	
PASSWORD	
NOTE	

WEBSITE	
USERNAME	
PASSWORD	
NOTE	

WEBSITE	
USERNAME	
PASSWORD	
NOTE	

Z

WEBSITE	
USERNAME	
PASSWORD	
NOTE	

WEBSITE	
USERNAME	
PASSWORD	
NOTE	

WEBSITE	
USERNAME	
PASSWORD	
NOTE	

WEBSITE	
USERNAME	
PASSWORD	
NOTE	

WEBSITE	
USERNAME	
PASSWORD	
NOTE	

WEBSITE	
USERNAME	
PASSWORD	
NOTE	

WEBSITE	
USERNAME	
PASSWORD	
NOTE	

WEBSITE	
USERNAME	
PASSWORD	
NOTE	

WEBSITE	
USERNAME	
PASSWORD	
NOTE	

WEBSITE	
USERNAME	
PASSWORD	
NOTE	

Note

Note

Note

Note

Note

www.ingramcontent.com/pod-product-compliance
Lightning Source LLC
Chambersburg PA
CBHW051435150726

48000CB00005B/2113